SUMMER FESTIVALS

Mike Rosen

Seasonal Festivals

Autumn Festivals
Winter Festivals
Spring Festivals
Summer Festivals

Cover: The Sugar Cane Harvest Festival, Barbados.

Editor: Geraldine Purcell
Designer: Ross George

First published in 1990 by
Wayland (Publishers) Limited
61 Western Road, Hove
East Sussex, BN3 1JD, England

British Library Cataloguing in Publication Data
Rosen, Mike 1959–
   Summer festivals.
   1. Festivals
   I. Title
   394.2

HARDBACK ISBN 1-85210-949-1

PAPERBACK ISBN 0-7502-0942-9

Typeset by Rachel Gibbs, Wayland
Printed by G. Canale C.S.p.A., Turin

Contents

Summer

Summer days are long, with early sunrises and late sunsets. Most people enjoy the warm weather but in some areas the hot weather can cause a shortage of water. When it rains there is sometimes a thunderstorm. Just before a thunderstorm the air feels thick and sticky with moisture. Then, with flashes of lightning and rolls of thunder, the storm begins. Large, heavy drops of rain crash against the ground so hard that they seem to bounce into the air as they splash. Summer storms can be fierce but they are normally quite short. Afterwards the air feels fresh again and everything glistens as the hot sun shines on the wet ground.

For farmers, summer is a busy time when many crops are being harvested. Many

Below **This field of sunflowers, growing in Pakistan, makes a splendid summer scene.**

Left The power and beauty of summer lightning can be a spectacular sight.

Below Harvesting summer crops, as shown here in a vineyard in France, provides jobs for students and seasonal workers.

farmers use harvesting machines, but in some countries the harvest is still gathered by hand. A lot of people are needed to work at harvest time. Sometimes people from neighbouring farms take turns to help with each other's harvests. The harvest may also be collected by workers who have been hired just for that short time.

Many people who work in towns and cities look forward to long summer days and fine weather to enjoy the outdoors. In the evenings and at weekends they may play sports, visit parks or eat picnics in the countryside. Many people like to spend time with their friends or visit another country for a relaxing holiday. Summer is the best season for holding festivals in the open air. People celebrate the strength of the sun and the growth of their crops, as well as important events in their country's history.

The Start of Summer

Long ago the Celtic peoples of Europe split each year into just two seasons – winter and summer. The Beltane festival, held on 1 May, celebrated the start of summer. As at all other Celtic festivals, bonfires were an important part of the ceremonies. When Christianity spread across Europe the purpose of this May festival changed. The farmers of Europe began to use it to celebrate the coming season when their crops would ripen and their livestock grow fat on good food.

Below **The tradition of erecting a Maypole for the May Day festivities carries on in this Austrian village.**

Despite the changes in the reasons for holding a May festival, many of the traditional dances and ceremonies of Beltane continued to be used. One such custom was the making of what in Britain is called a Maypole. Early in the morning, people would go to the nearest woodland and cut down a tree. It would then be stripped of all its branches until only the main trunk was left. This was then dragged back to the town in a procession.

When the procession reached the main open space, perhaps the town square or the village green, long ribbons of brightly coloured cloth would be tied to the top of the tree trunk. The trunk would then be lifted up and supported so that it stood straight once more, ready for the dancing to begin.

Above **May Day events such as Maypole dancing, are colourful and fun occasions to mark the beginning of summer.**

May Day Dances

Maypole dancing was traditionally done by women. Each holding one of the coloured ribbons they circled the Maypole with a hopping, skipping step. Some of the women danced in one direction while the others danced the opposite way round the pole, changing their direction at carefully chosen moments. As they danced, the women passed each other, sometimes on the outside of the circle, other times on its inside, until the ribbons were plaited together and wrapped tightly around the Maypole. This shortened the length of ribbon left to dance with and the circle of dancers moved closer to the pole.

Above **Morris dancing is a popular May Day spectacle, especially in Britain.**

When the circle was as small as it could be, the dance was reversed and the ribbons unwound until the dancers came back to their starting places. This dance around the Maypole may have reminded people of the way the hours of daylight shortened in winter then grew longer again as summer came.

Morris dances, traditionally performed by men, were supposed to frighten away the evil spirits of winter so that the summer could bring a good harvest and plenty of food. Morris dancing is based on very old European traditions. Some morris dancers darken their faces with mud and wear white costumes hung with rattles, bells and leaves. As they dance they stamp, clap and clash sticks together in time to the music. Some may wear animal masks during the dance, and there is often a 'hobby horse' – a man dressed as a horse.

Below **The 'hobby horse' man is often the centre of attention in May Day parades such as this one in Cornwall, England.**

The Workers' Holiday

At the end of the 1780s great changes were taking place in Europe, many of which began in Britain. New machines were invented for making cloth and the power of rivers and steam engines was used to drive the new machines. Factories were built where many machines could be operated together. People left their homes in the countryside to work in the factories and live in the cities which grew up around these new workplaces.

By the middle of the nineteenth century, many people lived in huge cities, filthy from the smoke and dust of the factories. They worked long hours without holidays and for very low pay. To improve their conditions these people joined together in trade unions and slowly the factory-owners were forced to give them better pay and shorter working hours. In 1889 an organization of workers decided that

Below **In the eighteenth century the new, expanding cities were smoky and dirty but people from the country needed jobs in the factories.**

there should be a public holiday each year on 1 May.

Since then, 1 May has become a special holiday for workers in many countries. In Britain the members of trade unions and other workers' groups hold parades and sports meetings. A very famous May Day event is the Durham Miners' Gala, held in the north of Britain. Led by brass bands playing traditional tunes the miners walk in procession, each group behind its own banner. These banners are decorated in great detail with scenes from the mining unions' history. Parades are also held in all the main cities of such countries as China and the USSR, where May Day has become an important national holiday.

Above **There are fabulous May Day celebrations, including fireworks, each year in Beijing, China.**

Dragon Boat Festival

As summer passes, fruits and berries appear on trees and bushes while the crops grow tall in the fields. In many countries water is scarce at this time of year. Festivals may be held which remind people how vital food and water is to their lives.

In early June the Chinese celebrate such a festival of food and water. It is based on a story which is thousands of years old. The story is that a man called Ch'u Yuan drowned himself in a lake to protest against his Emperor's cruel treatment of poor people. The dragons and evil spirits of the lake raced to consume Ch'u Yuan's body, but the local people

Above **Dragon Boats are skilfully carved and decorated to make a fantastic sight.**

tried to bring it back to shore to give it a proper funeral. To distract the dragons and spirits they threw rice dumplings into the lake. While the greedy spirits fought over the rice dumplings the people searched for Ch'u Yuan's body. They never found it and the Emperor was so sad when he heard the tale that he stopped his cruel ways at once.

Today the Dragon Boat Festival is an exciting event full of noise and colour. Boat races are held, each boat decorated with a painted dragon's head. While a drum beats out the rhythm, teams of rowers race their boats across the water to the finish. After the race there is a feast with many delicious foods. Among these are rice dumplings wrapped in bamboo leaves. The dumplings are filled with cashew nuts, spiced meats, fruit, or duck eggs.

Below **The effect of such decorations on the Dragon Boats can be very dramatic.**

Solstice Celebrations

Thousands of years ago people knew that the sun was vital to their lives. They depended on it for warmth and light. The sun's light helped them to hunt for food and grow crops. Many people worshipped the sun as a god.

At the summer solstice, hours of daylight are longer than at any other time of year, and the sun seems at its strongest. Sun-worshippers knew that after the summer solstice the sun's powers would seem to weaken as the days grew shorter and the nights lasted longer.

The Celtic peoples of Europe celebrated the summer solstice with bonfires, torchlit processions, and huge feasts. Their solstice festival was held to protect themselves and the sun from the evil spirits they believed were

Above **This is an Inca sun-god mask made of gold.**

present at that time. The details of their ceremonies are no longer known but they may have included prayers, dances and the sacrifice of animals. Similar celebrations took place in the ancient Inca and Aztec Empires in South America.

Today very few people celebrate the solstice, but some small festivals are still held by people who are keeping the old traditions alive. Some of these people call themselves sun-worshippers, or Druids after the ancient Celtic priests. In Britain, Druids have gathered for many years at Stonehenge in Wiltshire to watch the sunrise after the solstice.

Above **This old engraving depicts a Druid solstice ceremony at Stonehenge.**

Opposite **Some Peruvians still re-enact the sun-worshipping ceremony at the ruined Inca fort of Sacsahuaman.**

O-bon

O-bon is an important festival for Japanese Buddhists, which is celebrated in the middle of July or August. This festival honours the spirits of dead friends and family. Over the three days of the O-bon festival Japanese Buddhists welcome the spirits of the dead back into the family home for a joyful celebration. In order that all the family can be together at this time, many people return to their family home for this festival.

On the first day of the O-bon festival the family will go out to clean and tidy the graves of their ancestors. When they return home, herbs and flowers are placed on the household shrine to welcome the spirits into the house.

Above **Japanese families like to gather together for the O-bon festivities.**

At each meal over the three days of O-bon, food will be set aside for the spirits.

The second day of O-bon begins with a time for thought about the fate that awaits the spirit after death. Buddhists believe people's spirits are reborn after their death and go to a better or worse life depending on their past behaviour. Sometimes ceremonies are performed which will give the spirit better luck in its new life. Later on the second day people join together with other families for dancing and a celebration meal.

O-bon ends on the third day, when fires are lit to guide the spirits on their journey home. Sometimes these fires are built on rafts and left to float away on rivers or out to sea.

Below **Some Japanese women performing a traditional O-bon dance.**

Chung Yüan

Chung Yüan is another festival which honours the spirits of the dead. It is held in August, on the fifteenth day of the seventh lunar month in the Chinese calendar. At Chung Yüan everyone joins in honouring the unhappy spirits of people who have no family to remember them at other festivals, or those spirits who did not have a proper funeral. They believe that unless someone honours these spirits, they may cause trouble for everyone.

As at the spring festival of Ch'ing Ming the spirits are offered gifts that will be useful or make them wealthy – houses, clothes, money and food. These objects are drawn on paper and burnt in a fire so that the flames can carry the gifts to the spirits. In some Buddhist temples large paper models of boats are burned. These boats are believed to help the spirits cross the sea of pain which lies between them and a peaceful resting place.

Boats are also a feature of another Japanese festival, called Miyazu Toro Naghi, held in August. It is mainly celebrated on the coasts where many people work in the fishing industry. Lanterns in the shape of boats are floated out to sea as the evening tide goes out. The tide will carry the lanterns to the spirits of drowned sailors to help them to find their way home.

***Opposite* Chung Yüan is sometimes called the Festival of Hungry Ghosts. Buddhists believe that they should burn paper offerings, as shown here at a grave in Malaysia, to help the spirits of dead people be at peace.**

Independence Celebrations

Above **The fall of the Bastille marked the beginning of the French Revolution.**

Until the twentieth century, wars mainly took place in summer. This was partly because most roads were just dirt tracks which turned to deep mud in winter, stopping armies from travelling easily. Armies needed to travel at a time of year when there would be plenty of food in the fields and woods to feed the soldiers. The cold months of winter were a bad time to be on the march.

Many wars in the last two hundred years have been fought by people who wanted independence – the right to choose their own government. Because these wars were usually fought in the summer they are often commemorated by exciting, national summer festivals of independence.

The French Revolution started in the summer of 1789 as hungry people crowded the streets of Paris. The King and Queen of France offered no help to the starving people and anger grew when the poor saw the rich living in luxury. On 14 July 1789, thousands of angry people attacked the Bastille prison and set the prisoners free. As the revolution grew stronger the rulers of France fled from Paris in fear, and a new government was set up. On 14 July each year the French people celebrate the events of 1789 with parties and public firework displays. In 1989, on the 200th anniversary of the French Revolution, the centre of Paris was the scene of a magnificent pageant of French history. Many thousands of people in historical costumes marched through the streets in an enormous parade.

Below **The 1989 Bicentennial celebrations of the French Revolution included a magnificent firework display around the Eiffel Tower, in Paris.**

Independence and Freedom

Left **This painting depicts the signing of the Declaration of Independence, 4 July 1776. From left to right: John Adams, Roger Sherman, Philip Livingston, Thomas Jefferson and Benjamin Franklin.**

Many wars of independence were fought against foreign rulers. In 1775, people living in the British colonies in America protested at the way they were ruled by the government in London. One year later, on 4 July 1776, they declared their independence, promising to fight the British rather than accept their laws any more. After seven years of fighting the British gave up and the colonists in America set up their own government.

American Independence Day celebrations on 4 July are now one of the USA's biggest festivals. There are huge parades with marching bands, cheerleaders and decorated floats. In big cities like Chicago and New York the parades are showered with long streamers of thin paper called ticker tape. The weather is nearly always fine for the 4 July and many people eat their evening meal in the open air, often at friendly street parties, before going to a public fireworks display. As the explosions of the fireworks set the sky ablaze with colour

Below **Fireworks over Washington DC to celebrate Independence Day.**

and noise people celebrate late into the night.

Just to the north of the USA, Canada also celebrates independence from British rule, on the first Monday in July. In 1867, Canada was lucky enough to win its independence without a war. The celebrations are just as exciting as those in the USA, with parades, parties and special performances of plays and concerts.

Left **The Statue of Liberty, which stands on Liberty Island in New York Harbour, was a gift from the French people in 1886. It is often regarded as the symbol of the independence of the USA.**

Celebrating a New Start

In Australia, 26 January is celebrated as Australia Day. People remember the first arrival of colonists from Britain in 1788. On 6 February each year New Zealanders celebrate the Treaty of Waitangi which ended the wars between colonists and Maoris in 1840. Because the seasons are reversed in the southern hemisphere both these festivals come in the middle of their summer season.

Many countries in Africa and Asia celebrate freedom from the various European countries which ruled them in the past. Angola and Mozambique celebrate the freedom they won from Portugal in the 1970s, while North African countries such as Algeria and Morocco remember their struggle for independence from French and Spanish rule. Other

Below **The Bicentennial Australia Day in 1988 was marked by the entry into Sydney Harbour of a fleet of sailing ships, re-enacting the arrival of the first European settlers in Australia.**

countries which celebrate independence from British rule include India, and the African states of Ghana, Nigeria, Kenya, Uganda and Zimbabwe.

These independence festivals are celebrated with parades, speeches from government leaders, private parties and public firework displays. Often they are also occasions for protest by people who are unhappy with their government. The Maoris in New Zealand, Aborigines in Australia, and the Native Americans in the USA demonstrate to remind people that the colonists took land which was once theirs. In countries that contain people from many different religions there are sometimes protests from groups who feel their beliefs are not being protected properly by the government. Independence days are a good time to think about freedom for all the people who live in a country.

Above **Maoris in New Zealand performing their Action Song. Maoris are very proud of their culture and keep many of the old traditions, as do the Aborigines of Australia and the Native Americans of the USA.**

Eisteddfod

An Eisteddfod is a festival of poetry, song and music. Each year hundreds of these festivals are held in Wales, mainly during the summer. A similar festival called a Feis is often held in Ireland. During an Eisteddfod individuals and groups compete in contests to find the best writers, composers and performers.

One of the largest Eisteddfodau is the National Eisteddfod. At the National Eisteddfod nearly all the competitors are Welsh and the competitions are held in the Welsh language. There are special competitions for children or adults who are still learning to speak or write in Welsh. There

Above **Many countries send representatives of their national folk dancing to attend the International Eisteddfod, such as this group of Rumanian folk dancers.**

26

is also the Urdd Eisteddfod which is held just for young people. These Eisteddfodau give Welsh people a chance to show pride in their language and history. Some people wear the traditional Welsh national costume when they visit the National Eisteddfod. In these ways they keep alive the ancient customs which are an important part of Welsh history.

The International Eisteddfod at Llangollen is unusual because many of the competitors do not speak Welsh. Some are people whose families once lived in Wales but now live in other countries. Because of the many different languages spoken by the competitors the main competitions are for dance and music.

Eisteddfodau are part of a long tradition among Celtic peoples to hold a festival in the summer which brought them together in peace. When the Celts ruled Britain, many centuries ago, summer was the main season for fighting wars. A summer festival gave Celts time to forget their quarrels and enjoy themselves instead.

Left **These young girls are taking part in the crowning ceremony of the National Eisteddfod.**

Notting Hill Carnival

The carnivals in Rio de Janerio, New Orleans and the Caribbean islands are famous all over the world for their brilliant parades of costumed dancers and exciting music. Carnivals started many centuries ago as Christian festivals which began the period of Lent. They are held in January or February – winter months in those countries where Christianity had developed.

For such countries as Brazil and the Caribbean the weather is warm in January and February. When people from the Caribbean came to live in Britain in the 1950s they found that Carnival occurred in the coldest part of the British winter. Although they celebrated Carnival with parties in their homes and churches, they missed the fun

Left **Everybody tries to make sure the Notting Hill Carnival is a lively, colourful and happy event.**

Left **There are always some very elaborate and fantastic costumes worn during the Carnival.**

of their traditional open-air summer celebrations.

Many of the people from the Caribbean lived in the area of London called Notting Hill. In 1961 they decided to bring back their summer festival and held the first Notting Hill Carnival at the end of August. Although taken away from its Christian origins and dates it was a great success, and has been held every year since. The Notting Hill Carnival is now one of London's most exciting festivals. As at other carnivals throughout the world, there are pageants and parades of decorated floats and costumed dancers. In the sidestreets there are parties until late in the night, with plenty of food and music.

Glossary

Aborigines The original people who have lived in Australia since before the European settlers arrived.

Celtic The celts were people who lived in Europe and Britain in pre-Roman times.

Composers People who write music.

Independence Being free from the control of other people. Countries are independent if they have their own government instead of being ruled by a foreign power.

Legend An ancient story, often telling of important historical events.

Lunar A word used to describe anything that is related to the moon.

Maoris The original people who have lived in New Zealand since before the European settlers arrived.

Native Americans The original people who have lived on the continent of North America since before the European settlers arrived.

Pageant A parade in which people dress in historical costumes, and have floats that show events from the past.

Revolution When the people of a country rebel against their government and overthrow it.

Shrine A sacred place where people worship a particular god, goddess, or other object of devotion. A shrine can also be a chest or cabinet, built to hold religious relics.

Solar A word used to describe anything related to the sun.

Solstice The two times of the year when there is the greatest difference between the hours of daylight and the hours of night-time. At the winter solstice the day is shortest; at the summer solstice the day is longest.

Books to Read

These books might be of interest to you. You can get them through your local library. Ask the librarian to help you to find them.

Aborigines, by R Holder (Wayland, 1985)

Buddhist Festivals, by J Snelling (Wayland, 1985)

Carnival, by J Mayled (Wayland, 1987)

Festivals and Customs, by R Purton (Basil Blackwell, 1983)

Festivals Around the World, by P Steele (Macmillan, 1983)

Hindu Festivals, by S Mitter (Wayland, 1985)

India Celebrates, by J W Watson (Garrard, Illinois, 1974)

Jewish Festivals, by R Turner (Wayland, 1985)

Maoris, by G Wiremu (Wayland, 1984)

Plains Indians, by R May (Wayland, 1986)

Sikh Festivals, by S S Kapoor (Wayland, 1985)

Summer, by R Whitlock (Wayland, 1986)

Picture Acknowledgements

The publishers would like to thank the following for allowing their pictures to be reproduced in this book:

Celtic Picture Agency 26, 27; Eye Ubiquitous 8, 9, 19; Mary Evans Picture Library 15, 20; Sally & Richard Greenhill 13; Hutchison Library 14 (left); Japanese National Tourist Organization 17; Frank Lane Agency 5 (left); The Mansell Collection 10; Tony Morrison 14 (right); Christine Osborne 4, 28; Photri 6, 16, 22 (both), 23, 25; Spectrum Colour Library 24; Topham Picture Library 5 (right), 11, 21; Tim Woodcock 7; ZEFA 12, 29. All artwork is by Maggie Downer. Cover Eye Ubiquitous © Mike Alkins.

Index